W9-BWG-929

FACE TO FACE WITH

FROGS

by Mark W. Moffett

NATIONAL
GEOGRAPHIC
WASHINGTON, D.C.

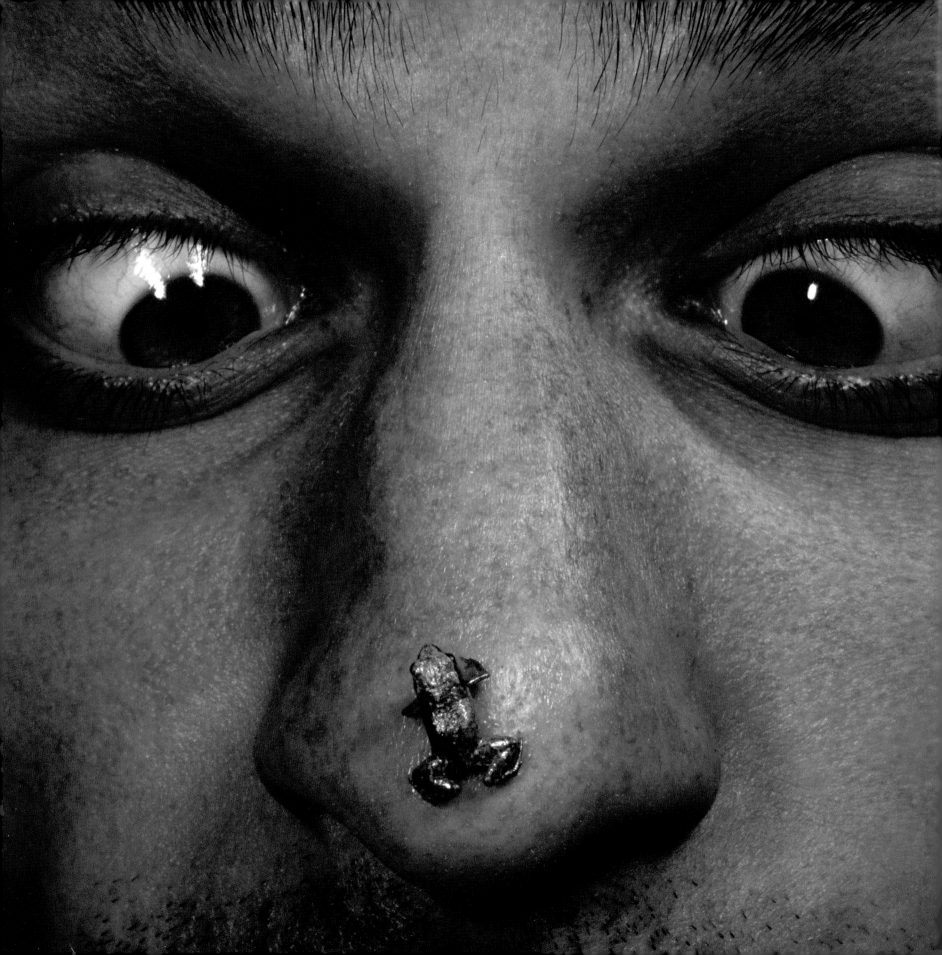

Everyone calls me "Doctor Bugs" because of my passion for small creatures—like this terribilis *frog in Colombia.*

FACE TO FACE

Are you good at catching critters? That's what I do. One time I looked for the smallest frog, which lives in the leaf litter in Brazil. My friends and I went through dead leaves one by one for three muddy days, just to find a single frog the size of the tip of your nose. I often go on frog adventures like this one, especially when I am on assignment for NATIONAL GEOGRAPHIC magazine.

My favorite frog adventure took place in a remote valley in Colombia, South America. There's a frog

Frog expert Fernando Mendez is shown with the world's smallest frog, which he helped me find in Brazil. People who study reptiles and amphibians, including frogs, are called herpetologists.

→ *The skin of the inch-long* terribilis *frog is covered with glands that secrete poison.*

FROG VS. TOAD

Don't be fooled. Toads are frogs. They are from a family of frogs called Bufonidae. In North America, these frogs adapted to drier conditions and became known as toads. What makes a frog a toad?

▬ Takin' it easy—toads tend to walk, not leap or jump.

▬ Warts and all—toads have drier, more warty skin than frogs.

▬ Armed and dangerous—many toads have poison glands behind their eyes.

in that valley scientists call *terribilis*—meaning "the terrible one." The frog got its name because its gold skin is so poisonous that a single touch can kill. It belongs to a group of frogs called poison dart frogs. *Terribilis* is the most poisonous of them all.

The frog lives a long way up a river in thick rain forest, in the land of the Embera Choco Indians. We had to paddle a dugout canoe to a village to ask the chief for permission to enter the frog's valley. One of the Indians made the blowguns his people used for hunting, and his teeenage son Paulino took me to the valley. When the boy found a frog, he gently rubbed a thin wooden dart over her moist back. The frog was fine, but now there was enough poison on the dart to kill an animal more than a year later.

The next day I went hunting with Paulino. He was very good at aiming the long blowgun. After he killed a wild pig (called a peccary), Paulino threw out the part of the meat that had frog poison on it—

6

it would make people sick. But the rest would make tasty pork chops for his village.

I had to lie on the ground with my camera only two inches away from the *terribilis* frog to take her picture. Compared to most frogs, she was curious, showing little fear. If you are deadly, you don't have much to be frightened of. Sometimes she hopped toward me, but I couldn't allow her to touch my skin. It was strange to be scared of such a pretty frog!

Always wash your hands after you handle any frog. But if you visit the rain forest, never ever touch a poison dart frog! Still, the poison isn't all bad. It keeps frogs safe from predators and can be used as medicine to reduce chronic pain in people.

Paulino takes aim with his blowgun. A single puff of air can shoot the dart many yards, as straight as an arrow.

MEET

Tree frogs like this species from Peru are good climbers because they have wide pads on their toes that are quite sticky.

THE FROG

I took pictures of this little guy at a tree stump in Panama. He was the toughest male dart frog around. When any other male dart frogs entered his territory, he would tackle them until they went away.

Frogs are amphibians—vertebrates that live part of their lives in the water. Like another group of amphibians, the salamanders, frogs have moist skin, and they drink and breathe through their skin when they are in water. Unlike salamanders, adult frogs do not have a tail, and their back legs are powerful for jumping. There are more than 5,400 kinds of frogs and toads around the world. Only about 104 of them live in the United States.

Frogs catch their prey with a sticky tongue they

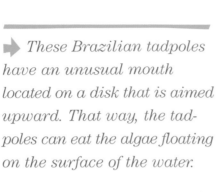
➡️ *These Brazilian tadpoles have an unusual mouth located on a disk that is aimed upward. That way, the tadpoles can eat the algae floating on the surface of the water.*

JUMPING FOR JOY?

— **Tree frogs are North America's jumping champions. But the longest jump ever recorded was 7.45 feet (2.27 meters) by the Australian rocket frog. Longer jumps have been claimed.**

— **Not all frogs can jump. Toads are terrible jumpers, and the African walking frog only walks.**

— **Jumping frogs store energy in springy tendons, which attach muscles to bones. The energy is released when the frog slingshots off the ground.**

throw forward out of their mouths. It can reach a third the length of their body. That's long—imagine being able to lick your belly button with your tongue! Most frogs eat insects, but the American bullfrog often swallows other frogs, and some huge tropical frogs eat mice or birds.

After frogs hatch from eggs, they undergo a kind of development called a metamorphosis. Like a butterfly that begins life as a caterpillar, a newborn frog goes through a period when it looks very different and eats and grows a lot. At this stage a frog is called a tadpole or pollywog.

Tadpoles live in water and have gills like fish. But unlike fish, they have a chubby body and a long, flat tail. For their first few days, most tadpoles hide and eat very little. Then they begin to use their tiny teeth to scrape off slime that grows underwater on rocks and plants. Their microscopic plant food is called algae.

The red-eyed tree frog from Costa Rica normally lives high in the trees, coming to the ground only to breed. Because it weighs so little, it cannot be hurt if it falls.

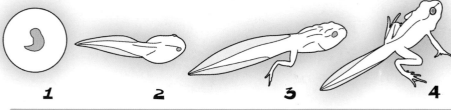

1   2   3   4   5

Most frogs follow a standard life cycle: An egg **1** hatches, and an aquatic tadpole that has a tail and breathes with gills **2** swims free. As it grows larger, it sprouts first legs **3** and then arms **4**. Losing its tail and gills during this time, it transforms into an air-breathing adult frog **5** that can leap in and out of water.

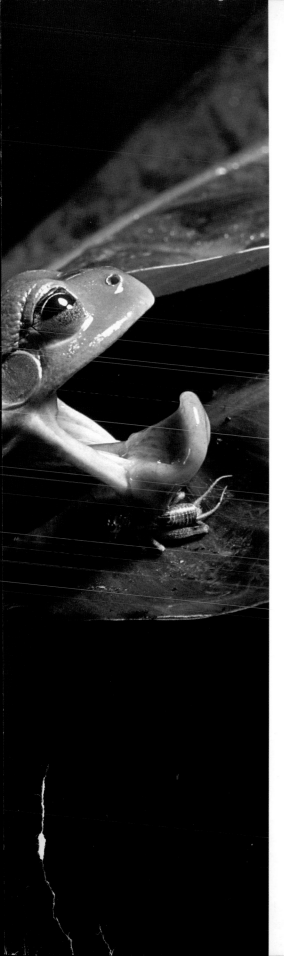

Some kinds of tadpoles turn into predators after a few weeks, when they are larger. Then they begin eating insects, or even each other.

As time passes, the tadpole begins to look more like a frog. First it sprouts little hind legs, then arms. The tail starts to shrink as it is absorbed by the body. By the time the little frog can first hop on land, it may still have a tail stub, but soon that disappears as well.

Many North American frogs live for several years. To survive the cold in the winter, they have to hibernate, burying themselves in the leaf litter on land or burrowing in the mud underwater. In hot weather, frogs need to protect themselves from drying out. Certain desert species stay underground until the rains come. I have seen an African frog that attaches to plants when the temperature rises over 100 degrees Fahrenheit (about 40 degrees Celsius). It turns white and stays as hard as a rock until the rains come. Then it absorbs water and hops away.

A frog's tongue is attached to the front of its mouth. The frog throws its tongue forward to catch an insect, like this cricket.

NOT YOUR

The coqui frog from Puerto Rico parachutes out of the trees every morning to avoid predators. By keeping its arms and legs outstretched, it slows its fall and lands on its feet.

AVERAGE FROG

This frog from Vietnam looks like a stone. As long as it doesn't hop, you would never see it hiding in plain view on the forest floor.

I'm lucky to have seen so many wonderful frogs. In Vietnam, I saw frogs that look like moss or a leaf, and in Brazil, frogs that dance. I've seen African frogs that look like they are covered with hair, Surinam toads in South America that suck in fish like a vacuum cleaner. I've seen frogs from Sri Lanka that eat leaves, and ones from Brazil that eat fruit. In Cameroon, I held a goliath frog that weighed six and a half pounds (almost 3 kilograms). Now THAT was a big frog!

I found a lot of cool frogs in the Atlantic Forest of Brazil. The dancing frog **1–2** lives in waterfalls so noisy that it dances rather than sings, stretching one leg and then the other, while wiggling the toes on the opposite foot. A pumpkin frog **3** enjoys a good fight—even with its own reflection. The fruit frog **4** lives in a sandy habitat where there are few insects— perhaps for that reason it is the only frog known to eat fruit.

Let me tell you a story about one of my favorite frogs, the coqui of Puerto Rico. As many as 10,000 coquis can pack themselves into just one acre, which is the highest concentration of frogs in the world. Male frogs sing "coqui" all night, and there are so many of them, they make a lot of noise!

During the day, coquis sleep in the cool shade near the ground. Each evening the frogs climb into the treetops to feast on insects. But their journey up the tree trunks is dangerous. If they climb when it's still light, birds catch them. When it's dark, tarantula spiders on the tree trunks are awake, and tarantulas love frog for dinner too!

It turns out there is a short period of time, just as it gets dark, when it's safe for coqui frogs to climb—after most birds fall asleep but before the tarantulas wake up. At that time all the frogs go up the trees together. When they've had their dinner and night is over they come down again, but that's easy. Coquis are only an inch long and light, so they aren't hurt by a fall. That means the little frogs can save time on their commute—and avoid their enemies—by jumping. Imagine it! For 15 minutes each morning all over Puerto Rico, it rains frogs...everywhere.

HOW TO SING LIKE A FROG

— You'd be a better croaker if you had the right equipment. Most frogs have inflatable vocal sacs that make really loud calls—even louder than birds 100 times their size!

— Frogs have different kinds of calls for different reasons—courtship calls, warning calls, or just, "Hey, I'm over here!" calls.

— When frogs in a species sing at once, it's called a chorus. See if you can form a frog call chorus with friends. Happy croaking!

17

DEADLY FROGS

Dart frogs are some of the best mothers in nature. In Panama, the female strawberry dart frog lays her eggs on dry ground, in the leaf litter. This becomes a problem after her eggs hatch into tadpoles—a tadpole needs water! Luckily, mom stays with her babies and can come to the rescue.

As I watched one mother, a tadpole wiggled onto her and held tight. Dart frogs normally stay on the ground, but with a tadpole attached to her back—as if in a baby backpack—she hopped to a

↑ *There are over 250 species of dart frogs from Central and South America. Many of the most beautiful ones are classified in the genus* Dendrobates. *A favorite is the blue poison dart frog* D. azureus *which lives in a remote part of Surinam: Here two females are fighting* **1** D. speciosus **2** *lives in a mountainous region of Panama near Costa Rica. The red-headed dart frog from Ecuador and Peru* **3** *has my favorite species name:* fantasticus, *meaning "the fantastic one." Pictures* **4, 5, 6** *show dart frogs from Bocas del Toro, a small group of islands in Panama. Though the frogs look different from one another, they all belong to the species* D. pumilio, *the strawberry dart frog: Each island has a unique color. Some people try to collect the more color-ful dart frogs for pets, but taking too many animals from the wild could threaten the species with extinction.*

◀ On Taboga Island in Panama, there are many green-and-black dart frogs and many tarantulas. Most of the time, they seem to avoid each other. Every once in a while, I saw a tarantula foaming at the mouth, apparently dying from having accidentally bitten a dart frog.

tree and began to climb for the first time in her life. This wasn't easy for her, because dart frogs do not have the big sticky toe pads that frogs who live in trees have. But slowly and surely, mom and baby went higher and higher up the tree trunk.

What was she looking for? In the rain forest, plants called bromeliads grow in trees. They look like pineapple tops. Puddles of water form between the plant's spiky leaves. The mother frog found a bromeliad and climbed into one of these

↑ *Biologist Kyle Summers climbs a rope to follow a male green-and-black dart frog. In this species it's the father who finds canopy ponds for his tadpoles.*

➡ *Some dart frog species carry all of their tadpoles on their backs at once, like this one from Ecuador.*

ponds. Her tadpole slid off her back into the water. That tadpole had its own, private swimming pool. Then mother climbed back to the ground to pick up another tadpole. She would be very busy that day, because she had to put her twenty offspring in pools scattered in different trees and bushes.

Why would a mother frog go to so much trouble just to give each of her tadpoles a separate place to live? Because a tadpole's life is dangerous. It turns out that while adult dart frogs are poisonous, their tadpoles are harmless and tasty. Many animals want to eat them. By keeping her young in different places, the mother doesn't put all her "eggs in one basket." A snake might eat one or two of her pollywogs, but he probably won't find them all.

After the mother frog gave each tadpole a home, she returned to the ground. She hopped around and ate ants, her favorite food. (In fact, the dart frog's poison comes from the ants. If a frog doesn't eat enough ants, it loses its poison.)

Three days later, the mother frog began climbing all those trees once again, remembering exactly where to find each of her tadpoles. And were they happy to see her! When she arrived, each tadpole

A tadpole holds onto its mother's back, looking like a human baby on a piggy-back ride.

wiggled its tail in the air as if to say, "Hi, mom!"

After the tadpole waved, the mother did a curious thing. She backed into the pool and laid an egg in the water. This egg is not fertilized. It's like an omelet—a little meal for the tadpole. Humans give their babies milk, but dart frogs feed their tadpoles omelets.

Every few days the mother returned to each tadpole to feed it another egg. Gradually, within a few weeks, the tadpole grew legs, then arms. Finally it lost its tail. It was now a little dart frog, ready to move out of its pool and eat ants.

The mother's ability to remember where she hid her tadpoles is amazing. No one thought a frog was smart enough to do such a thing until biologists started to watch the dart frogs very carefully. It was then we discovered that a dart frog can be a great parent.

Plenty more discoveries await us in the fascinating world of frogs. Come—explore them with me.

HOW YOU CAN HELP

⬇ *The largest frog is the goliath frog from West Africa. These children in Cameroon hold a six-and-a-half pounder.*

Frogs can live successfully in virtually every environment on Earth, but so can humans, and sometimes that's a problem. Every time a wetland or swamp is drained or a forest cut to make way for development, frogs lose out.

In fact, dozens of species have gone extinct recently, and other populations are severely threatened. Most of these extinctions can be tied in one way or another to human activity.

Frogs breathe and absorb water through their skin, so they are particularly vulnerable to chemicals and pesticides. This makes them environmental markers of a sort—a way to measure the environmental health of an area. When pollution affects an area, frogs are often the first to die out.

Climate changes, such as global warming, produce altered conditions that can weaken frogs. This makes them more likely to catch diseases.

In recent years, the biggest disease threat faced by frogs is the chytrid fungus, which attacks frogs' skin and makes it difficult for them to breathe. It can spread easily and quickly and wipe out whole populations. Here's how you can help:

▬ Work with your family and friends to preserve natural spaces in your area. A natural space with frogs living in it is probably a healthy natural space.

▬ Clean water and unpolluted land are good for frogs. So do your part to conserve resources: If you have a backyard, compost your kitchen scraps; don't waste water and energy; recycle. Every little bit helps.

▬ Keep reading about frogs, and learn everything you can about them. Maybe do a school project on saving frogs. Share what you learn with your family and friends.

▬ You and your family could also contribute to one of the many groups working around the world to save frogs, such as the Rainforest Action Network or the World Wildlife Fund.

IT'S YOUR TURN

USE YOUR EARS, NOT JUST YOUR EYES.

Finding frogs can be tough. Although some frogs like to come out and sun on lily pads, other frogs are harder to spot. But their calls give them away, even at night.

Each type of frog has its own call. Spring peepers welcome spring with a deafening chorus. Run your finger quickly across a comb—that's what a chorus frog sounds like. The green frog's call sounds like a plucked banjo string, and wood frogs, like a duck with a cold.

Your assignment is to listen, track, tally, and record these sounds for yourself.

1 First, study and plan. You can listen to hundreds of frog calls on the Internet *(see Find Out More, page 30)*. Find out what frogs are in your area and what they sound like.

2 Next, plan your frog listening adventures. You could go to a swamp or pond with an adult who can tell a peeper from a bullfrog. Or have your family check out your local nature center—they often offer woodland tours, sometimes at dusk.

3 Listen carefully. Do you hear peeps? Trills? Barklike sounds?

Make a chart of the different sounds and tally them. Bring your chart on each trip, and compare and contrast what you hear at different times of day. Are frogs louder and more active at dusk? How about in different seasons?

4 If you have a recording device (often a cell phone can record sound), record the frog calls. Try to identify the frogs you hear with the help of field guides and the Internet.

Careful! Some large frogs like this Brazilian species can give you a bad bite.

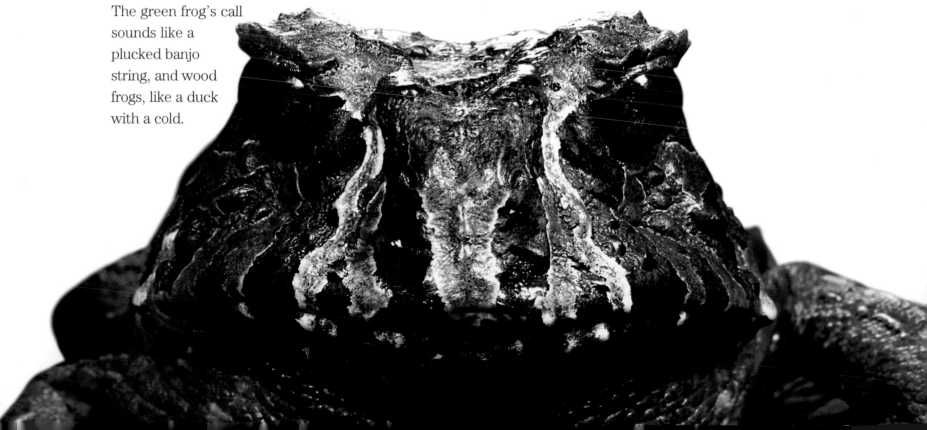

FACTS AT A GLANCE

⬇ *The world's largest gliding frog is from Vietnam. Though its outstretched toes slow its fall, the frog still lands with quite a splat.*

Scientific Name

People use common names to refer to frogs, but these can differ around the world. Scientists try to use the same name to refer to a species, no matter where they are. This is called its scientific name. For example, scientists call the *terribilis* frog *Phyllobates terribilis*. Frogs and toads are in the zoological order, or animal grouping, Anura.

Types of Frogs

There are roughly 5,422 different frog species in the world.

Reproduction

In most frogs, after mating, the female releases her eggs into the water while swimming, and the male fertilizes them. Frog egg masses form clusters in ponds and lakes. Most toads lay their eggs in long strings in shallow waters, such as the puddles in tire ruts. When frog eggs hatch, tadpoles (or pollywogs) emerge. Some frogs lay their eggs on land, and the tadpole stage takes place inside the egg. When those eggs hatch, tiny frogs pop out and hop around.

Lifecycle

Tadpoles breathe through gills, have long flat tails, and live underwater. As they grow, tadpoles begin to develop legs, lose their gills, and develop lungs—at this stage, tadpoles often break the water's surface to gulp air. Their bodies then begin to absorb their tails, their eyes grow much larger and shift position, and their legs grow stronger. Soon, the young froglets—some still sporting tails—lug themselves onto land to begin life as a frog.

Lifespan

In captivity, small frogs have survived from one to five years, and bullfrogs have lived for 15. One European common toad is reported to have lived for 40 years. However, little is known about the lifespan of frogs in the wild; it's most likely half that of captive frogs. In general, the larger the frog, the longer the lifespan.

Habitat and Range

Frogs and toads live in every environment on Earth except

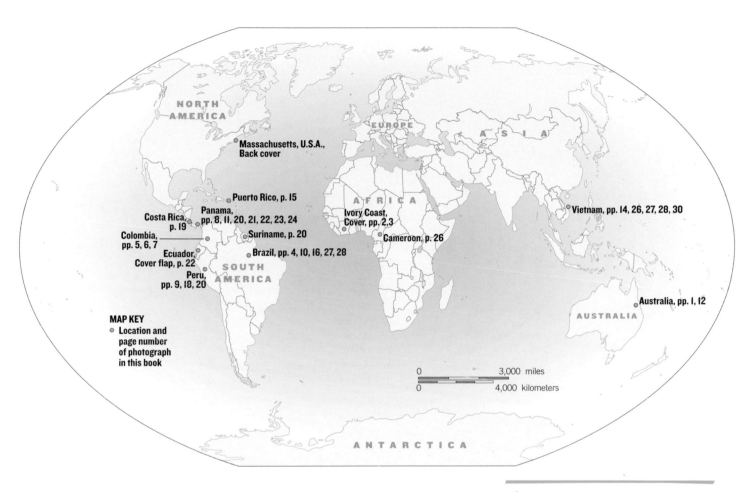

MAP KEY
○ Location and page number of photograph in this book

Massachusetts, U.S.A., Back cover

Puerto Rico, p. 15

Panama, pp. 8, 11, 20, 21, 22, 23, 24

Costa Rica, p. 19

Colombia, pp. 5, 6, 7

Suriname, p. 20

Ecuador, Cover flap, p. 22

Brazil, pp. 4, 10, 16, 27, 28

Peru, pp. 9, 18, 20

Ivory Coast, Cover, pp. 2, 3

Cameroon, p. 26

Vietnam, pp. 14, 26, 27, 28, 30

Australia, pp. 1, 12

0   3,000 miles
0   4,000 kilometers

those that are frozen year-round. Frogs' main requirement is access to water. They can be found in swamps, small ponds, streams, forests, mountains, and even deserts. Frogs don't like saltwater and have trouble getting to remote islands in the ocean. The highest living frog lives in the Andes at an elevation of 17,717 feet (5,400 meters).

Diet

Small tadpoles eat algae or microscopic animals. Adult frogs are carnivorous—they eat almost anything that moves that can fit into their mouths, including insects, worms, slugs, snails, small mammals, and even other frogs.

Biggest threats

Human activity (elimination of

⬆ *Frogs live on all continents—except Antarctica.*

wetland and forest habitat; pollution from chemicals and pesticides); climate change; introduced predators (such as non-native fish); and the chytrid fungus, a mysterious disease that can wipe out whole frog populations.

GLOSSARY

algae: microscopic plants eaten by many tadpoles.

amphibians: vertebrates that live part of their lives in water and part on land. There are three types of amphibians: frogs, salamanders, and caecilians (which resemble worms or snakes and mostly live underground).

bromeliads: tropical plants in the pineapple family; some frogs live or lay eggs in the pools of water that accumulate at the base of the leaves.

herpetologists: people who study reptiles and amphibians.

metamorphosis: the developmental changes a frog goes through, from egg to tadpole to adult.

tadpole: the early stage in a frog's life when it lives underwater, breathes through gills, and has a long, flat tail.

toe pads: the pads on the bottom of the feet of tree frogs that enable them to stick to leaves and climb easily.

vertebrates: animals that have a backbone.

FIND OUT MORE

Books & Articles

Behler, John L. and Behler, Deborah A., *Frogs: A Chorus of Colors*, Sterling Publishing, New York, 2005.

Behler, John L., and King, F. W., *National Audubon Society Field Guide to North American Reptiles & Amphibians*, Alfred A. Knopf, New York, 1995.

⬆ *Staring down the Vietnamese moss frog*

Web Sites

AArk (the Amphibian Ark project)
http://www.amphibianark.org/

American Museum of Natural History
http://www.amnh.org/exhibitions/frogs/

Amphibiaweb
http://amphibiaweb.org
To listen to frog calls: http://amphibiaweb.org/lists/sound.shtml

Australian Museum Online
http://www.amonline.net.au/herpetology/faq/frogs.htm

Conservation International
http://www.conservation.org/xp/amphibians/index2.xml

Declining Amphibian Populations Task Force (DAPTF)
http://www.amphibians.org./index.php

Frogland
http://allaboutfrogs.org/

Frogs: A Chorus of Colors (exhibit)
http://www.reptiland.com/exhibit.html

GAA (Global Amphibian Assessment)
http://www.globalamphibians.org/

The Philatelic Frog (frogs on stamps)
http://www.philatelic-frog.fr

Rainforest Action Network
http://www.ran.org

U.S. Department of the Interior, U.S. Geological Survey
http://www.pwrc.usgs.gov/frogquiz/index.cfm?fuseaction=main.lookup

World Wildlife Fund
http://www.wwf.org